Paint

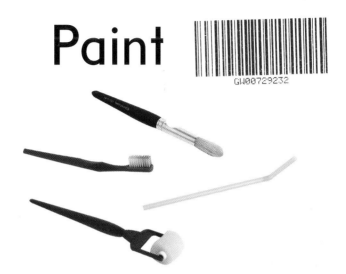

Written by Julie Ellis

Photography by Michael Curtain

HORWITZ
MARTIN
EDUCATION

Look at me.
I can paint
with a paint brush.

Look at me.
I can paint
with a straw.

Look at me.
I can paint
with a toothbrush.

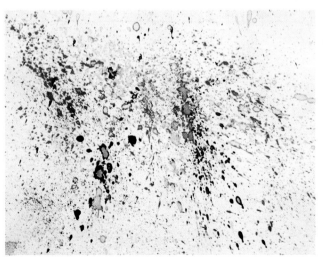

Look at me.
I can paint
with a roller.

Look at me.
I can paint
with my hand.

Look at my paintings.